NEW Spirals

Diary of a Wild Thing

Angela Griffiths

Text © Angela Griffiths 2001

The right of Angela Griffiths to be identified as author of this work has been asserted by her in accordance with the Copyright, Designs and Patents Act 1988.

All rights reserved. No part of this publication may be reproduced or transmitted in any form or by any means, electronic or mechanical, including photocopy, recording or any information storage and retrieval system, without permission in writing from the publisher or under licence from the Copyright Licensing Agency Limited. Further details of such licences (for reprographic reproduction) may be obtained from the Copyright Licensing Agency Limited, 90 Tottenham Court Road, London W1T 4LP.

First published in 2001 by:
Nelson Thornes Ltd
Delta Place
27 Bath Road
CHELTENHAM
GL53 7TH
United Kingdom

01 02 03 04 05 / 10 9 8 7 6 5 4 3 2 1

A catalogue record for this book is available from the British Library.

ISBN 0-7487-6063-6

Cover artwork by Richard Johnson
Typeset by Tech-Set Ltd, Gateshead
Printed and bound in Great Britain by Martins The Printers Ltd, Berwick upon Tweed

1

Friday, 1 August

This morning I went to the market and bought this diary. It was dead cheap. I need to keep a diary. It might help me to stay sane. I have a problem. A mega problem. I think I'm turning into a WEREWOLF!

Help! Help! Help! Why are parents never around when you need them? Mum and Dad are away in Spain. Living it up. They won't be back for another 12 days. By then they probably won't know me! I could be just a dark shape prowling about at night.

I must face facts.

Fact number one – this evening I stood at the window and gazed at the moon. Why?

Fact number two – when I was cleaning my teeth I looked in the mirror and saw wild eyes staring back at me.

Fact number three – my sense of smell is much stronger than usual. My socks stink!

Fact number four – the backs of my hands are suddenly quite hairy.

The facts add up to one thing. The dreaded curse is upon me! This could be all my own fault. If only I hadn't poked about in Dad's room. That's where I found the spooky old book that used to belong to his Grandad. It's a book about weird and wonderful legends. It has lots of pictures, including a picture of a werewolf with red eyes. Scary! No wonder Dad hid the book away.

After I first looked at the book I let an hour go by. Then I went back to have another peep. This time I saw a picture of a werewolf with bared teeth! I wish I hadn't seen that picture. I'll probably look the same soon!

This evening I watched boxing on television – and I don't even like boxing. I thought it would help to take my mind off things, but it didn't.

Mum has left little yellow stickers all round the house. Here's what I've found so far:

'Don't forget to turn off the cooker.'

'Don't forget to water the pot plant.'

'Don't forget to clean your teeth.'

'Don't forget to be polite to people.'

'Don't forget to wash up.'

'Don't forget to worry.'

That last one was meant to be funny. My mother has a really odd sense of humour. My father is the only one who understands it.

Tomorrow I'll see my girlfriend, Amy. I'll do my best to act normal. She must never, ever know about my problem.

This diary must be kept TOP SECRET. In the end I may have to burn it – or eat it.

2

Saturday, 2 August

I didn't sleep much last night. Worry kept me awake. How long before the world knows my dark secret? At three o'clock in the morning I found myself in the bathroom – talking to myself in the mirror. On my way back to bed I saw a shadow on the wall. It was not my shadow. It had large pointed ears!

A card arrived from Mum in Spain. She wrote, 'The weather is here. Wish you were fine.' That's her idea of a joke. I hope the postman didn't read it.

I stayed in all morning. I did a lot of deep thinking. What will happen at the next full moon? Will I really turn into a werewolf? What have I done to deserve such a fate? Why me? I had a bath and sloshed on loads of Dad's new aftershave. It will help to cover any wolfish smell.

Amy called at two o'clock. She was keen for us to go to the town's annual show. She said it was bigger than ever this year. The posters called it 'A Fun Day Out'. I agreed to go. I thought a fun day out would help to take my mind off my problem. How wrong I was!

Things were all right to start with. Amy and I strolled round the stalls, chatting in the sunshine. She bought candyfloss for herself and gave me a big bag of popcorn. I bought a pink key ring with the message, 'Be My Valentine'. It was ever so cheap. I gave it to Amy as a present for her birthday tomorrow.

At three o'clock we went to the main ring. We managed to get front row seats. Amy bought a programme. It listed all the events:

1 Motorcycle Display Team.
2 Heavy Horse Parade.
3 Vintage Cars.
4 Carriage Driving.
5 Country Dancing.

I enjoyed the first event. But when we got to the second event – the heavy horse parade – things went wrong. Badly wrong!

The shire-horses were led into the ring by their owners. Their brasses were gleaming. Everyone clapped. Amy and I leaned on the rail and waited for the horses to trundle past. All you could hear was the slow plod of hooves and the jingle of harnesses – until the horses came near me.

When the horses reached the place where we were sitting, they stopped. Their mood changed. They began to sniff the air and stamp their hooves. They backed away and rolled their eyes. They shook their heads and sent spittle flying into the crowd. One of the owners lost his bowler hat. It got flattened – flat as a pancake.

The man on the PA system said, 'Ladies and gentlemen, we are sorry about this upset. These gentle giants are usually very calm. Perhaps one of them has been bitten by a horsefly.'

After the horses were led away, Amy said to me, 'Are you all right?' I fixed a grin on my face and nodded. But I nodded a lie. Really, I was worried about what had happened. The horses had been fine until they came near me. Then they seemed scared. SCARED OF ME!

The next event – the vintage cars – came and went. I hardly noticed them. Then Amy asked me again whether I was all right. I turned on her. 'Yes! Yes! Yes! Of course I'm all right!' I felt awful.

Things went from bad to worse. I was dreading the next event – the carriage driving – because there would be more horses. I tried to get away.

'Amy, I need to go,' I said.

Amy gave me a look. She grabbed my arm and told me I had to wait. She said we'd paid good money for our show tickets. She hates wasting money.

So I sat rigid and waited as a carriage and four brown horses came into the ring. The scene looked perfect. The driver was in period costume. He had the four horses fully under his control – until they came near me.

As soon as the leading horse drew near he became jittery. He sniffed the air and jumped about. This upset the other three horses and the driver pulled hard on the reins. The lead horse stared at me. Then it flattened its ears and snorted through flared nostrils. It swished its tail and tried to rear up!

Some children sitting near us thought this was part of the act. But it wasn't. It was for real. The driver no longer had control. The horses ran out of the ring, and then out of the exit gate. The carriage was no longer stately. It looked more like a war chariot!

The man on the PA system said, 'Ladies and gentlemen, the horses seem to be having an "off" day. This is most unusual. We do apologise.'

I stood up and rushed away from the ring. Amy followed. I told her I was going home. She said she would come with me. I think she was worried about me.

On the way home, Amy said, 'You're not yourself today, are you.' I asked her what she meant. She said, 'You are so tense. Is something bothering you?'

I said, 'Yes, something is bothering me – but I can't tell you about it yet.'

Then she said, 'You smell funny today. Why is that?'

I thought the moment of truth had arrived. I thought she was going to say I had an animal smell. But then she said, 'Are you wearing aftershave? It smells the same as my Dad's. He gets it cheap from the market. It stinks!'

As we walked through the town we saw lots of barriers set up. Police were still trying to catch the runaway horses. Some farmers were trying to help. I kept well away.

I wanted Amy's opinion about what had happened at the show. So I said, 'Amy, the show horses didn't seem to like me. Please tell me what you think.'

She just stared at me. *'I* like you – so don't worry about what horses think.'

Before she left, Amy told me what her gran had given her for her birthday. It was two tickets to the zoo. We are going there tomorrow – and I'm dreading it! The zoo will have wolves!

3

Sunday, 3 August

What happened today was worse than what happened yesterday! I'm still recovering. If things get any worse I could crack up!

Amy arrived soon after breakfast. I wished her a happy birthday. Then I told her that I wasn't keen on going to the zoo. She said, 'You'll enjoy it when you get there.' I could only think WOLVES!

I told her I hadn't slept well. I said I needed to stay at home and catch up on my sleep. She looked at me with her big blue eyes. She said, 'Did you mean it when you wished me a happy birthday?'

I said, 'Yes, of course I meant it.' She then told me that it would only be a happy birthday if we both went to the zoo. If we didn't go, she would have an unhappy birthday.

What could I say? I tried to look on the bright side. As we left the house I felt as if I had a date with destiny. Perhaps I was *meant* to go and meet my hairy brothers. So we went.

The first hour at the zoo was all right. We saw lions, tigers, giraffes and camels. I let Amy think I liked looking at wild animals. But all the time I was worried that I *was* one!

I think Amy could tell I felt tense. When we were looking at the giraffes she tried to make me laugh. I said, 'I wonder why giraffes have such long necks?' She said, 'They need long necks because their heads are so far away from their bodies.' I fixed a grin on my face, just to please her. Her sense of humour is a bit like my mother's – pathetic.

Soon after that we walked near a signpost saying 'Wolf Pit'. I tried to walk on past. But Amy stopped to read the noticeboard about wolves. She read the facts out loud to me. 'Wolves are very intelligent. They hunt in packs. They do not chew their food. They tear it and swallow it in chunks. They can easily gulp down a whole mouse. They must have fresh meat or they die.'

I agreed with the bit about wolves being intelligent. But the last bit made me shiver and shake!

I made myself look down into the wolf pit. One of the wolves looked up. He was a silver-grey colour. He was the largest of the pack, probably the leader. He stood still, dead still, and stared at me. He began to wag his tail. Then he sank down and rolled over onto his back. I think he was trying to send me some kind of signal. The thought scared me rigid.

I turned away and the wolf gave a howl. A loud, blood-curdling howl! He did one howl after the other, hardly stopping for breath. Soon, all the other wolves joined in!

My legs felt like jelly. I sat down on a bench. Then Amy started chatting to a zoo keeper. She asked him why the wolves were making such a noise. He told her they were doing a Big Howl. He said they must have picked up the scent of something.

Did he mean something or someone? My mind couldn't cope with it all. I wanted to go and join in the chat but I didn't trust my legs.

The zoo keeper had his hair in a pony tail and he wore a gold ring in his ear. I don't know what he said next, but Amy started to giggle. I felt left out. The more he looked at Amy the more I felt like throwing him to the wolves!

After a few minutes I called to Amy. I said I had a pain in my belly (true) and I wanted to go home. We left the zoo soon after that.

On the way home I could see that Amy was upset. She said she had wanted to visit Pets' Corner. I told her we could go back some other time. She made me promise, and that annoyed me. I said, 'Why do I have to promise? Can't you take my word for it?'

She looked surprised at my outburst. She said, 'All right, there's no need to snap.'

I said, 'Look, if I say we'll go back to the zoo, we'll go back! OK?'

She said, 'There's no need to bite my head off.'

When she said that, I wanted to tell her about my problem. But I didn't – and I'm glad I didn't. She wouldn't understand. And who could blame her?

For the past hour I've been sitting on my bed, worrying. I keep thinking about that big silver wolf at the zoo. The way he stared at me. The way he wagged his tail. The way he rolled onto his back. And the way he led the Big Howl. I really do think he was trying to bond with me. Yes. It takes one to know one!

4

Monday, 4 August

Bedtime should be the most relaxed time of day. I remember reading that in a magazine. What a joke! I feel as relaxed as a spring under a mud wrestler's mattress!

I wish I'd stayed indoors this morning. If I'd stayed in, I wouldn't be feeling the way I feel now.

I was stupid. I missed breakfast and rushed out to visit the new supermarket in Stony Street. It was the first day and they were giving away free offers.

I had a look round. But most of the free offers were boring. Who wants oven cleaner, soap powder, that sort of thing? As I was leaving the store, a woman handed me a sample pack of dog biscuits. We don't have a dog, but I took the biscuits. This turned out to be a bad move!

There were three flavours of dog biscuit. T-bone, Topside and Tripe. On the way home I thought about these flavours and my mouth began to water. I wondered which would taste best. I nibbled the first biscuit. Then the second. Then the third. Yummy! Before I knew it, I'd scoffed the lot!

After this I felt sick. Sick with worry. What normal person would eat a dog biscuit? What normal person would *enjoy* eating a dog biscuit?

I was halfway home when I noticed an Alsatian dog following me. He followed me all along Clink Street. Then along Wine Street. Then through the churchyard.

I started to trot. Then I began to run. But the beast kept pace with me. I put on a spurt and ran as fast as I could. He was close behind, making little 'yip-yip' sounds. I could tell he was enjoying the chase!

I reached home just in time. Another minute and I dread to think what might have happened! As soon as I was indoors I fell on all fours. I was panting and dribbling . . . like a wild thing.

What a good thing Amy didn't see me acting like that. Now I have to ask myself, why did the Alsatian follow me? Was he attracted by the smell of dog biscuits – or could he detect the smell of WOLF? I have just been sniffing my arm. As a test. I could be wrong, but the smell seems to be more animal than human.

What will my parents say when they come home? How will I break the news to them? 'Mum, Dad, I'm sorry. I am not your dear son any more. I am half man, half wolf.' I wonder how they will take it. Will Mum fall to the floor, sobbing? Will Dad cry out, 'My son! We love you, no matter what!'

On the other hand, they might not believe me. They might just laugh out loud. That's more likely. Just my luck!

Groan! I have just seen in my diary that there will be a full moon on Saturday. HELP! A full moon! Only five days away!

5

Tuesday, 5 August

The day began with a bad sign. My nose felt cold and damp! I remember reading in Dad's spooky book that people change slowly. Stage by stage. They only become fully werewolf when there is a full moon. Time will tell!

I had a strange dream in the night. In my dream I was a handsome silver wolf. I was running beside Amy and she was making 'yip-yip' sounds. We ran through a forest until we came to a tree with round yellow flowers. Under the tree was a huge wolf with a ring in his ear. He growled at me. Then we began to fight. It was a fight to the death. I woke up just in time. My heart was pounding.

The weather has turned very warm. It's the start of a heatwave. I felt restless all morning so I went to the library. I wanted to find out more about werewolves.

Things went wrong as soon as I stepped inside the library. I heard a story being read aloud to a group of kids. The story was Red Riding Hood! I heard all about the big bad wolf's terrible teeth . . . and sly eyes . . . and jaws and claws.

No wonder I panicked. I ran through a doorway. But it was a staff door, and this set off an alarm bell. It took ages for the staff to find the key to turn off the alarm. Everyone stared at me. I wasn't popular.

A member of staff offered to help me. She asked what sort of book I wanted. I didn't dare to say that I wanted a book on werewolves. So I said, 'Give me any sort of book about wolves.' She soon found a book for me. It was about timber wolves and how they mark their territory.

As I was leaving the library the senior staff member gave me a funny look. She was speaking on the telephone. She may have been speaking to the police – or even the RSPCA!

At five o'clock Mr Trout from next door came round. He invited me to tea with him and his wife. I told him I was busy. I don't mind his wife, but he gets on my nerves. He used to be a keep fit instructor in the army. He retired ten years ago, but he still wears a tracksuit and a whistle. He does press-ups in his garden every morning of the year. Just showing off.

I was glad to see the back of him. He has a funny smell. Lots of things have a funny smell. Funny smells are all around me. It's all part of my problem.

Only another wolf would understand.

I have spent most of this evening prowling about the house. I read a page of my library book. I weigh exactly the same as a young timber wolf. That thought almost put me off my food. But I managed to eat two Pot Noodles, followed by a pizza, followed by instant mash and a currant bun. The wrapper of the bun said it had 25 currants. I didn't bother to check.

I have tried to read my palm. My lifeline looks a bit short. I'm sure it's much shorter than it used to be. So far there are no hairs on my palm. That's good.

What a good thing I have this diary! Writing helps me to stay sane. I wish I knew the future. If I am a werewolf, how will I cope? I have taken a vitamin pill. If the worst happens, at least I'll have a glossy coat. One thing is for sure. Life is a wilderness.

6

Wednesday, 6 August

Eleven o'clock. The end of a long day – and I'm at the end of my tether.

The day started all wrong. When I was washing my face I looked in the mirror – and FIERY eyes were staring back at me. Not only that, my eyebrows seemed thicker than usual. Perhaps my eyes were red because I hadn't slept much. I tried counting sheep, but that only made me dream of chasing them!

At ten o'clock this morning Amy called round. She begged me to go with her to visit her Gran. 'Please come,' she said. 'It could be fun.'

I agreed to go. Fun didn't come into it. We argued all the way to her Gran's house. The argument was about the way I looked.

'Why are you wearing dark glasses?' she asked. I didn't know what to say. I wore the shades to cover my fiery eyes.

Amy said, 'Some people look cool in dark glasses, but you're not one of them.' I tried hard to think of a cutting reply. Deep down inside I think I wanted to bite her.

Amy wasn't the only one to object to my new look. When Amy's Gran opened the door she frowned at me. It wasn't exactly a warm welcome. Amy led the way into the front room and I sat down. Amy kicked me. I can take a hint. I removed my shades.

The next thing I heard was hissing and spitting. I knew Amy's Gran didn't like me – but this was going a bit far! But then I found a cat under my chair. Hissing and spitting. Even clawing!

'What's wrong with Fluffy?' asked Amy.

Her Gran said she couldn't understand it. 'Fluffy is always a calm cat,' she said. 'Fluffy only gets upset when she's near a dog. Fluffy hates dogs!'

This was another sign! I turned hot and cold. I was really glad when Amy's Gran took the cat outside. When Amy's Gran came back she said I was sitting in the cat's own chair. She said that could be the reason for Fluffy being upset.

We left soon after that. I was glad to get away – right away from Fluffy. That cat stirred up feelings in me – primal feelings I'd rather not name. I think cats that blow hot and cold are stupid. What is the point of them?

At lunchtime Amy and I shared a bag of chips. She said she was sorry for being rude about my shades. I realised then that I'd left the shades at her Gran's. Just as well. Some things are meant to be. When Amy and I said goodbye we were both in a better mood. I waved to her all the way down the street. It was quite romantic – until I backed into a lamp post.

My good mood didn't last long. I spent most of the afternoon worrying. Why was Fluffy so huffy? What did it mean? Did the cat smell wolf on me? Do smells rise like hot air? How long before birds attack me? By six o'clock I was worn out with worry. I decided to have a bath and try to relax.

In the bath I found extra hairs on my body. There are even a few on my chest! Worse was to come. As I was stepping out of the bath I found a flea on one of my legs. A FLEA! I captured it on a bar of wet soap.

It's another sign. I'm sure that humans don't get fleas as big and black as this one! How much more stress can I take? I'm not only going to be a werewolf. I'm going to be a *lousy* werewolf.

Tomorrow I plan to visit the local vet. Surely he'll be able to help me.

7

Thursday, 7 August

Today I went to the vet's. I can't think why I bothered. Things went wrong from the start. When I was in the waiting room a man arrived with a big dog. The dog's name was Rufus. He was a friendly dog. Too friendly! He kept on sniffing my hair. Then he licked my face and it felt like an electric shock. I asked his owner what breed he was. I should have known. Rufus was a WOLFHOUND!

When I went in to see the vet he was surprised to see no animal with me. When I took the soap box out of my pocket his face lit up. 'Aha!' he said. 'I like stick insects. They are such delicate things.'

I told him I hadn't got a stick insect. But he didn't seem to hear me. He went on and on about stick insects. He asked whether my stick insect had lost a leg. He asked what I was feeding it on. He said that privet leaves were the best food.

He looked shocked when I opened the soap box and showed him a dead flea on a bar of soap. He looked at the flea for a long time. Then he said, 'I'm sorry. There is nothing I can do for your pet flea. It's dead.'

I tried my best to look sad. Then I said, 'I need to know – is this the sort of flea that lives on a wolf?'

He gave me a strange look. Then he said, 'It's the sort of flea that lives on a common cat.'

I was on my way out when a girl rushed after me. She was the office girl. She handed me the vet's bill. I was very surprised. I didn't expect to have to pay for a lecture about stick insects! I gave the woman the few coins I had with me. Then I gave her the soap box in part payment. But it still didn't cover the bill.

'You'll have to do a bit of work,' she said. She handed me a broom and told me to sweep a long passage. She told me to be quiet because six dogs were getting over operations. While I was sweeping, one of the dogs began to bark. Then the other dogs began barking too.

There was such a noise that the girl went to look at the dogs. When she saw me she said, 'It's amazing! All the dogs are standing up, wagging their tails! I've never seen dogs recover so fast. They seem so happy!'

All the way home I thought about what had happened. I was glad for the dogs, but worried for myself. I still can't work it out. How did the dogs know that I was near? They couldn't see me. They must have been able to smell me. Perhaps they thought of me as one of the family. Perhaps they even thought of me as some kind of leader or protector.

I'm in bed now. Tired out. But I don't think I'll get much sleep. I'm too worried about the wolfish blood flowing through my veins. I have tried reading boring things in an effort to feel sleepy. Just now I looked at Yellow Pages. I think I've found a useful phone number. Tomorrow I'll get the help I need.

8

Friday, 8 August

It's late at night. The heatwave is still on. I feel fed up. Let's face it – I'm all alone in the world. Alone with my problem.

At nine o'clock this morning I phoned the number I found in Yellow Pages. It turned out to be a set-up called Happy Helpers. They might feel happy, but I thought they were a dead loss.

I spoke to a woman called Gloria. She said no problem was too hard for Happy Helpers. She said she wasn't easily shocked. Then she asked about my problem.

I told her I had the first signs of something – but I didn't say what. She said, 'You must go to your doctor without delay.' I told her that my problem wasn't medical. Not in the way she meant, anyway. I told her I had signs of turning into a werewolf. I could tell she didn't believe me. She told me off for wasting her time with a crank call.

It took about five minutes, but at last I got her to believe me. She changed her tune then. She said I mustn't worry, and I mustn't feel alone. She said there could be many people who kept their wolfish habits a secret. And who could blame them? Wolves have always had a bad press. She told me to get my worries off my chest and talk to someone. Stupid woman! That's what I was trying to do!

Amy phoned me this afternoon. She wanted to know why my phone was engaged this morning. She demanded to know who I was speaking to.

I told her it was a business call. She said, 'What sort of business?' I couldn't tell her, of course. She then accused me of chatting up other girls. She was sniffing a lot. I told her she was the only girl for me.

She wanted me to go with her to the cinema this evening. I asked what film was on. She said the film was called 'Once in a Blue Moon'. There was no way I could go with her. I was worried about the danger so late at night. What if I became a werewolf and bit her?

Amy reminded me of my promise that we would visit the zoo again. She still wants to see Pets' Corner. She began sniffing again. So I did the easiest thing. I agreed. It's all arranged for Sunday, the day after tomorrow.

This evening I did something a bit wacky. I did what wolves do to stay cool. I dug a pit in our garden. I was lying in the pit, trying it out, when Mr Trout looked over the fence. 'Are you all right?' he asked.

I told him I was training to be an undertaker. But that didn't get rid of him. He said, 'You should get out more. You need to see the funny side of life.'

I gave him a look. 'What funny side?'

He then asked whether I was interested in joining the local fishing club. I told him that I thought fishing was cruel to the fish and to the maggots. I remembered to be polite. (Mum would have been proud.) As I went indoors I said, 'I bid you goodnight.'

It's all right for people like him. They haven't got my worries. Tomorrow night there will be a full moon!

9

Saturday, 9 August

My nerves are in shreds. At the start of the day I overslept, so I got up late. I kept waking up in the night. It was so warm. I kept walking about the house. I had to open doors and windows to let some air in. Every time I fell asleep I had the same dream – which woke me up. In my dream I was running through tall grass, chasing a herd of buffalo. Amy was running with me. Her coat was shiny in the soft light of dawn. Her amber eyes were full of love. That was only in my dream, of course.

I may have walked in my sleep. When I opened the front door to take in the milk I saw a puddle on the path. I HOPE the puddle was nothing to do with me!

The postman delivered two cards from Mum and Dad in Spain. Mum's card had a picture of a donkey on it. She warned me not to act wild or wolf down my food. Dad's card had a picture of a Spanish dancer. He said he was enjoying the sun, the sand and the sea. He said he was going to speak to Mum about staying on in Spain for another week.

What about me? Nobody seems to care about me! Are my parents selfish or what? They seem to have all the luck. And all I get is problems. I remember when I was 5 years old. My friend and I both had loose teeth. When his tooth fell out he got money under his pillow. I swallowed my tooth when I ate an apple. Life is just not fair!

This afternoon I tried to prepare myself for tonight – the night of the full moon! I tried deep breathing while sitting with my legs crossed. My efforts to find inner peace didn't work. I ended up with split jeans.

Before it got dark I closed all the curtains and locked all the doors. Just for safety. I felt very restless and kept prowling about.

I had a bath (which I didn't need). Then I watched television. Then I ate cold leftover meat pie and pizza. Then I opened a family size bag of crisps. Then I ate cold leftover custard. Then I tried to do a crossword and felt cross. Then I watered Mum's pot plant, a bit late. Then I finished off the crisps.

Just after nine o'clock the doorbell rang. It was only Mum's friend, Jade, on her way to the local disco. She rang the bell three times. Then she called through the letterbox to say she had made me a jam roly-poly. I let her think I was out. She pushed the jam roly-poly through the letterbox. I ate most of it, then I felt strange. I don't think she's a very good cook.

Soon after that I went into the kitchen to get a drink. But I forgot that the kitchen doesn't have curtains. By mistake I looked through the window – AND SAW THE MOON!

Within seconds I felt as if a magnet was pulling me. Out of the house . . . out into the back garden. I stood and gazed at the moon for a long time. I felt weird, but strong, full of power. I can't believe what I did next. I leapt up onto the shed roof . . . and I gave a long, loud howl. AAAAAWOOOOOOOOOOOOOOO!

I was about to try another howl when someone hurled a boot at me. The boot hit me on the ear. I ran indoors, yelping.

10

Sunday, 10 August

I woke early with my face twitching and my legs on the run. I was drenched in sweat. As I rolled out of bed I hit my ear on the bedside table. Now I've got two sore ears!

As soon as I was up I saw that my bedroom window was open – wide open! I didn't open it, so who did? Could I have opened it in my sleep? Did I leap out? Did I spend the night prowling about all over town? If I'd had a wolf's night out I'd rather not think about it!

I kept my promise to Amy. We went to the zoo. But I told her I was only willing to visit Pets' Corner. On the way to the zoo I tried to have a serious talk with her. I said, 'Amy, tell me, have I got an unusual body odour?'

She just stared at me. She was puzzled. So I tried again. 'Have I got a doggy smell, perhaps?'

Then she was her usual blunt self. She said, 'The weather is hot. Anyone who wears the same T-shirt for over a week is bound to smell!'

At the zoo we went straight to Pets' Corner. Amy was smiling and talking non-stop. She loved every single living thing. She kept on saying, 'Oh look! How sweet!' Even when we stopped to look at some baby snakes she said, 'Oh look! How sweet!' I could tell she was in her element.

She insisted on using her new camera. She took a picture of me with a stinky ferret, then one of me with a nanny goat, then one of me holding a lamb. I dread it when that last picture gets developed. It will probably show me as I really am . . . a WOLF!

At midday I said, 'I'm so hungry I could eat a horse.' I wasn't thinking when I said it.

We stayed in Pets' Corner to have our picnic lunch. This turned out to be a big mistake! Things went wrong from then on. I was feeding a baby bat with my apple core when I heard a blood-curdling sound. It came from the other side of the zoo. It was a long drawn-out howl. The howl of a WOLF! I turned round, my hand jerked – and the bat bit me!

There wasn't much blood. But I soon felt faint. So we rushed to the first aid post. I don't think the nurse there was much good. She didn't do stitches or anything. She just stuck a plaster on my finger and said, 'It's only a nip, not a bite.'

I asked her what other treatment was needed. She said none. She said if I was worried I could go to my doctor and ask for a jab. I felt like giving her a jab. She had no feelings. Hard as nails. I felt like reporting her.

Amy came home with me. She made lots of hot, sweet tea for shock. Her shock. She said the house was a mess, worse than a pig sty. She reminded me that my parents are due back soon. She counted three old chip bags on the floor – but there was no need for such a fuss. 'You'd better chill out and get this house cleaned up,' she said. She can be really bossy at times.

All the time Amy was talking, I was flat out on the settee. I had my eyes closed. I was worried. Could the shock of the bat bite set off the werewolf thing? I did a few low moans to show I was in no state to do housework. Then I asked Amy to help me. She said no. She had to go home and help her Mum with housework.

A bit later I heard something drop through the letterbox. It was a note from Amy with a bar of chocolate. She said she was sorry she couldn't stay to help me. She hoped the chocolate would cheer me up while I did the housework. There was a PS at the end. It said, 'Why do you remind me of a squirrel?' I turned the note over. It said, 'You're both utter nutters!'

This evening I washed up some dishes and scraped the burnt bits from the frying pan. Then I went from room to room, flicking a duster. When I got to Dad's room, I tried not to look at the spooky old book. But I couldn't resist it. This time it fell open on a page about VAMPIRES! I stared at the picture. The vampire had a face as pale as chalk and he was hovering in mid air. SPOOKY! Oh, I wish I could turn back the clock. I wish I hadn't been bitten by a bat! Why? Why me?

I've just looked in the mirror. My teeth – top teeth, both sides – seem longer. Is this a sign of fangs? And are they wolf fangs – or vampire fangs?

I feel mixed up and out of sorts. Before getting into bed I stuffed garlic under my pillow. I've also put some in my pyjama pocket. You can't be too careful!

11

Monday, 11 August

It's three o'clock in the morning. I'm in bed. But I'm not asleep.

I've just written Amy a poem. If I have to go on the run, it will comfort her.

> Dear Amy, my friend,
> this could be the end
> of true love as you and I know it.
> But I'll see you soon
> by the light of the moon.
> Yours truly – a werewolf and poet.

I've been doing a lot of thinking about life and everything. I'm trying to work things out. *Really* work things out.

I must face facts.

Fact number one – I'm scared. Dead scared.

Fact number two – I HATE VAMPIRES. They must be the most feared creatures on earth.

Fact number three – I would rather be a werewolf than a vampire. At least a werewolf is only a werewolf some of the time.

Here is a list of things I would hate to be:

1 A vampire.
2 The Loch Ness Monster.
3 The Yeti (abominable snowman).
4 King Kong.
5 An alien from outer space.

Writing that list has helped me. I keep reading it. Then I say out loud, 'What a good thing I'm only a werewolf!' I say it over and over again. What a fool I've been! I mean, what's the big deal? In a funny sort of way I've got used to the idea of being a werewolf. The idea has grown on me . . . stage by stage.

It's strange. My mood has changed. I feel so much better. It's almost true to say I feel happy!

I've just done another wacky thing. I don't know why I did it. It wasn't planned. I stood at my open bedroom window and I howled. I howled at the moon. AAAAAWOOOOOOOOOOOOOOO! I think I was trying to prove something – but I'm not sure what.

Now it is four o'clock in the morning. I'm in bed, but still not asleep. I can hear the distant rumble of thunder. I can also hear a dog howling outside.

Now I can hear two dogs howling. Now three! Now four! Now more! A lot more! This cannot be. Am I dreaming?

Help! Help! Help! I have just looked out of the window. There are dogs outside. Or they could be hounds. Hundreds of hounds! Their red eyes are glowing in the light of the moon. They must have come from all over town. As soon as they saw me they stopped howling. They just stood with jaws wide open, wagging their tails. But why? Oh dear, I think I know why.

I must keep writing. My sanity hangs by a thread. I can feel panic rising. My mouth feels funny – saliva glands must be working overtime. My palms feel itchy. In fact, I feel itchy all over. Mustn't scratch. Scratching is bad for the coat.

I've had another peep out of the window. They are all still there. Are they dogs, hounds or wolves? I can't tell. They are waiting. Waiting. Silent now. I think they could be trying to send some kind of message. From their brain to my brain. 'Come on down. You are Top Dog. We need you. Come and lead the pack!'

What shall I do? Now they are howling again. It's an amazing sound. The howl of 100 hairy beasts. It's music to my ears! I think I'll join the song of my blood brothers. I must! We are all from the same family tree!

AAAAAWOOOOOOOOOOOOOOO!